this house,
my ghetto

This book is dedicated, with love, to
Marie, Bethan and Ciaran

this house, my ghetto

mike jenkins

seren

seren
is the book imprint of
Poetry Wales Press Ltd.
First Floor, 2 Wyndham Street
Bridgend, Mid Glamorgan
Wales, CF31 1EF

© Mike Jenkins, 1995

Cataloguing In Publication Data for this book
is available from the British Library

ISBN: 1-8541-140-X

All rights reserved. No part of this publication may be reproduced, stored in a retrieval system, or transmitted at any time or by any means, electronic, mechanical, photocopying, recording or otherwise without the prior permission of the author.

The publisher acknowledges the financial assistance of the Arts Council of Wales

Cover painting: 'Echoes' by Philip Childs

Printed by Redwood Books Ltd, Trowbridge

Contents

7	Always the Ocean
8	The Woods
9	The Lodger
11	Lessons
13	Doing Henry V
14	A Strange Recognition
20	Red Kite Over Heol Nanteos
21	Dream Meeting
22	Waiting for the Train that Never Comes
24	His Old Red Hillman
25	The Memory Dance
26	Blackberrying
27	Middle Age
28	Famous Player
29	Psychodahlia
30	Gurnos Shops
31	New Houses on Georgetown
32	Yn y Carchar
34	Yr Wyddfa Speaks Out!
36	Living on the Coastline
37	The Ghost Boy
38	National Thinking
39	Leaving
40	The Human Hatchery
41	Openings
42	Intruder
43	Diver-Bird
44	Sensing the Waun
49	Odd Bird
50	The Talking Shop
51	Catalogue for Those Who Think They Own Everything
53	Searching the Doll
54	Jasmina in the Snow

55 Vedran Smailovic
56 Beyond the Pale
57 Jack of Pumps
58 Anti-resort
59 Jesus Runs Wild
60 Man on a Skip
61 This House, My Ghetto
62 Dwr

64 *Acknowledgements*

Always the Ocean

For those of us born by the ocean
there will always be a listening,
an ear close to the ground
like an animal trailing.

I remember one night
I couldn't see anything of water
and I was sober as the stars,
yet below the tracked paving-stones
and gushing up through cracks...
benches tilted, clouds rocked.
I was a vessel, filled full of it.

This town at the valley's head
I've adopted or it's adopted me:
wakes fan from the simple phrases
and often laughter can erode
the most resistant expressions.
Despite this, I'm following the river
along our mutual courses:

to the boy on a storm-beach
hopping from boulder to boulder
trying to mimic a mountain-goat;
to the young man sitting in a ring
of perfumed smoke by the castle,
gazing at strings of dolphins
plucked by the sleight-fingered sea.

The Woods

Hacked through trees
the paths raced bare
of grass and weed,
were there before we came.

Each moment became the next one
except from the clearing,
where a ledge of earth
was look-out on a farm:

its high-wire fences protecting
an orderly world outside
our gorse-roofed dwellings.
Our talk of electric charges

burning you to ash
if you dared... dash, jump,
swing... the bramble scabs
and mud-patches on knees

would seep in, to make
a map of these woods
whose names were Burma, Apache-land,
whose buzzards spied for 'Nazzis'.

Every day we died many times.
Nettle-stings more painful
than falling down and counting out:
dock leaf emblem of our tribe.

The Lodger

The three children swooped on the letters:
dark-haired boy, eldest one, the dealer
flipping over a trump card
'Look! Look at his middle name!
I've never seen that before!'
With his sister, he guffawed
and flapped his prize, swatting
the laughs not to bring attention.
Youngest, left out, did a goalie's spring
to reach, but 'Here, have a look!'
Quickened by guilt he read 'Fitzgerald'
and it stuck, a curious nickname.

Tea-time was Fitzgerald's occupation
of the kitchen and the youngest
shrank his mam to a key-hole
as she spooned veg he couldn't name,
a waitress at the shoulder.
Unfamiliar and exotic smells gushed
through the door and their talk
went side to side, not in competition
but like levels of a building.
He thought of the earlier mockings
and wanted to be part of them,
to put in window-frames, to set
a river and pasture scene.

That was the year Kennedy died.
The older ones saw it on television
and expected the lodger to realise
the prophecy of his name and go away
with his suitcase full of samples,
leaving his collection of bottles
and their heavy hints of seduction.

But he remains there sitting, napkin tucked;
inflated from all her indulgence,
condensation covering his specs as their mam
crouches at the door, spying into a hall
of vanished children and letters falling.

Lessons

Peter and me, Morgan and Jenkins,
not knowing 'hiraeth',
not mourning mountains.

Bookends of a new terrace,
sons of the professional classes
losing accents to flatness.

Comparing how we pronounced it,
how far we could go
into 'Llanfairpwllgwyngyll....'

He went further than me,
frequently visiting grandparents
at a place called Tony Pandy.

I'd come a long way since 'Welshie',
'Taffy', learnt to squeeze my vowels
up the tube of my throat.

And on a school trip to Aber
I believed their stories of cave-dwellers
who'd be dressed in sheep-skins:

raided the local bakers, cunningly
hiding behind polite requests,
mocked at staying in 'Ruddy Penny'.

Wales was a big-dipper, breath-snatching,
or crumb-catching gulls by a half-pier:
a land of sent-away holidays.

I marked its black in Geography
like some tarred organs
and praised its industries.

Its Chartists marched for a sentence only
and then gave way to lists of taxes,
'Glendower was hot-blooded' I copied willingly.

Doing Henry V

Good King Harry called on us to fight the Frogs
and I had sympathies with his cause,
despising all that masculine and feminine
and declensions of verbs. I was chosen
to be at the breach of the teacher's desk,
to put on a stage-Welsh Fluellen:
it was tough as eating leeks
coughing up that accent
from years ago forgotten Aber
and my tongue slipped more
on the muddy heaps I built
than Shakespeare's verse I'd learnt to rack
like most Grammar boys blazered and badged.
I reddened to a rose at Fluellen's
daff-Taff mentality, wanting a voice
sharp as a lance, clear as a flag.

A Strange Recognition

Aberystwyth

A coincidence of eyes,
a lightning vision
across tables. Our notes
plodded, the out-of-date
statistics fixing us to seats.

Your long brown hair
I'd drawn in imagination
before we ever met.
My hungover head
too heavy to prop
juddered with the shock
of a strange recognition.

***

Outside the edge of the dance
I watched you ceilidh, swing
wildly with waves beneath your feet.

When we met I wanted to hide
in your accent, yet you mimicked me
as if learning a different language.

In the library, your metal-rimmed glasses
framed your eyes downward, concentrated.
Away from shelved knowledge
we barely touched, I noticed
their green of sea in a certain light.

***

Huddled and holding against the night-tide,
along the winding promenade,
stepping gradually into each other's histories.

The spurt and spume of breakers
hitting the sea-walls,
heat from our words making faces glow.

I rode the wind as I'd done
when a boy on the mountain:
then you caught me stumbling.

I lifted you up into air
which rolled and rounded our years
as beach-pebbles are eroded.

***

The day after, I talked
of someone else the next summer,
teasing you with her name
and letters exhibited:
cruel reminders of impermanence.

You didn't tear with spite,
but clung on so tightly
I wanted to throw your hand
out across the bay,
knowing it would come back eventually.

***

In your flat exchanging tales
of relatives, like well-worn books:
you took me across the water
before I'd boarded a boat.

I collected your sayings
pressed by our lips:
making the bulbs shake,
floorboards creaking fears.

Our minds were ceiling-cameras:
a film director we both imagined
yelling 'Cut... cut... cut!'
just at the crucial instant.

***

It was a long way down
from the grassy hollow
above the cliff, a fit for our bodies,
to a station platform
and chat about domesticities.

From the seagulls' calls sharp
as rock pinnacles, to a park duck
alighting on a fence so near
I faced it lens to beak!

There was no ring of stalks
to be knotted round your finger,
only a timetable to make,
shunting our agreement into place.

But wherever we clutched
we'd glimpse the edge
and a rough path ahead,
always wary of falling.

Belfast

All around us the city was turning
into dust with dark approaching:
white dust from fires,
black dust flaking from buildings,

churned into the air
by a worry of helicopters.

Nothing else seemed substantial there:
I snuggled close to your softness
and the sheets whispered.

I shrank in your shoulder's cusp,
drinking your milky tones,
parched with oppressive dryness.

All you'd taught me couldn't explain
the guns' long hollows
and the one deadly mistake.

**

You spoke for me in daylight.
I blocked off my throat
like the streets we encountered.
Though firesides flared banter, argument.

I searched for the right expressions
but you kept the map
inside your head,
aware of the worst threats.

Times I thought you'd hidden
the voice I needed
and I'd act the interrogator
to make you confess.

Before sleep, it knocked at my heart
to be let in and I knew then
why you leapt at an everyday explosion
of noise from door or pan.

***

A mat of cheques
on the Presbytery floor.

If only your tears
had made the ink run
and blur, become a fog
of figures for a puzzled bishop.

They sentenced us there,
gave us 'Twelve months! No more!'
They tore up our documents
as if that's all we were.

Your family owned one brick
of the parish church.
In a place where names and colours
could be a crime, we decided to make
our own banners and search
for a renegade who'd accept
the heresy of a love condemned.

***

I believe it was that first
union of looks, or further back
to that part of our selves
where opposites had been built:
good and evil, right and wrong,
brick above true contact's soil.

Not a vow or signature
nor legal paper with single name,
not a ring of precious metal
nor a hired suit for the occasion,

not a black limousine one citizen
rightly met with a two-finger salute.

Careless of your earnest whiteness
I wanted to strip the veil.
I was actor and commentator
at the stage of the altar.
Priests and congregation embraced
at the renegade's bidding.

What I want to remember is speeding
towards the border, joke-sprung,
lost in Free Derry in our rickety car;
towards a wilderness of coast and bogland,
heading for horizons as they surely darkened.

Red Kite Over Heol Nanteos

Walking with my brother over a chalk escarpment
our separate childhoods miles of years away,
though bracken reminds us of Penparcau:
huge prehistoric ferns
a cavern of fronds
to conceal you in hide-and-seek
till everyone had gone.

We leave our past with them
brown and flakey as old papers,
to follow paths by sycamores and beeches
by wind-sculpted oaks and precocious saplings:
talking two nations in a reservation
motorways have been told not to reach.

Laughter flies over the unmapped border
between us, his ears finely tuned
to birdsong which, to me, all merges into one.
He points out a willow-warbler,
common enough, yet its descending scale
is made virtuoso by his enthusiasm.

He tells of a red kite over Heol Nanteos,
circled in his sights
before he drove on.
Birds migrate for food and season,
he jets because of ambition:
exotic trilling and rainbowed plumes.
The red kite is rare, it is threatened,
so close to once our home.

Dream Meeting

Like a dead person, you visit me
in my dream. You'd received
my invitation and the lie you told
about it not existing will wake
with our miles-apart bodies in daytime.

Here, alive on a telegraph
of waves — we've inherited
from ancestors before any family names —
you enter. You're younger
than I expect: as if those useless
presents exchanged like unsaid insults
were lying in wait with alarms.

More vivid than a photograph,
with a child's power of magnification,
I draw in your face, seeing
the burst veins on your cheeks
our shared complexion and my nose
pointing at me like a fin.

In fierce but honest brightness
I keep this to tell my children.
It's all they have of you
except those curt penstrokes of 'Love'
sharp as a slap or a nod in passing.

I count the years and months of separation,
knowing my dream was childless,
knowing it was a conference in a vast
anonymous mansion with people all around us
to keep our tones groomed and precise;
knowing only sleep could arrange such a meeting.

Waiting for the Train that Never Comes

The walls without a picture
or a flourish of tell-tale stain,
doors always locked and windows
without a crack for air.
The waiting-room, a choke of chairs,
the stench of urine
stings the nose and tongue.
No-one serving as she sits
and knits her fingers,
her face a glare of bruises
where she'd fallen from her cot.
Too many pills for nurses to explain,
too many timetables and screaming
wheels without destinations.
We offer chocolates and she offers one
to a pleasant vase who could be going
in the same direction.

Emily Ellen in Wenvoe, fussed over
by big brothers, the smell of leather binding
stronger than bread rising:
demanding, demanding with foot-sore tantrums.
Helen in Barry, slight and pretty,
in the frame and facing out to sea,
courted and sung, teaching young children
whose hands crop and wave.
Nelly, married but away in Rutland,
train-line connection with her husband:
he'd walk her round and round
pleading for a 'Yes!' once again.
Aunty Nell, still in the classroom,
powdery as her own bread,
reciting morals and poems
with equal rectitude.

Gran with card-player's shade:
questioning doors to be let in
and clocks for never answering
and her grandson for letting strangers
use her home like some station.

His Old Red Hillman

He gave us his old red Hillman
rust-rimmed and hoarse-engined.

On a dipping Antrim road
it accelerated on its own
and there was his wilfulness
often drawn through the door
at noise of shooting, despite warnings.

Its radiator began to drip
and steam like a railway engine,
our box of bottles chinking
as we chugged over ramps:
annoying as his cackhanded ways,
his bricks and books to jack.

The lining hung off
where troops had rummaged for clues
after his gunpoint kidnap;
the upholstery flapped and waved
yet stayed stuck on:
so he returned, though nobody missed him.

Those bald remoulds we never checked,
haring towards drystone walls in a skid,
two inches from hospital: the irony
of his Dunlop's job while tyres
were left to themselves,
not cared for like children.

He was there in the many dents and bashes:
the buckled bumpers, the cracked mirror;
patiently taxiing neighbours to Mass,
his wife's illness buffeting within.
How the guttural exhaust
didn't scrape tarmac and fire sparks
I'll never know. So many routes
cordoned off, his split map couldn't tell.

The Memory Dance
(i.m. Philip Greagsby)

'Anything strange or startling?'
your catchphrase over the phone:
with few of the heavy steps
of your adopted home.

In an armchair, made higher by papers,
you sat under a blanket of print
snoozing with the radio on in case
something happened round the corner.

Your best friend, the ace reporter,
used to take you with him as scribe,
yet you never wrote us letters.
Now you're the only news that matters.

Leaving food to rot, the car's haphazard,
we drive off into the night
and encounter a frightened fox, dazzled:
his nocturnal sight we borrowed.

I cry as we descend the mountain,
the city so much less for your leaving.
I must meet you for the last time:
lying, not an ink-bruise to be seen.

Against tradition, we carry you, men and women
away from the path and over weedspread stones
away from communal plots whose names
you'd have tallied with a clerk's precision.

Ringing's no longer an ambulance siren.
Your elegant long-hand is waltzing
in your diary, to a gentler tone:
the memory dance has its own time.

Blackberrying

Clutching lunch-boxes but not working,
we're off to the Waun
clambering over the stile
wellied and lumbering
between summer and autumn:
sun warming skin, wind stiffening bones.

Hopping the frog-pastures
we hear the donkey's raucous brays
making our giggles small as sparrows
and see in the distance
a shine of horses: white and brown
and fawn and mottled.

'Where are we going?'
'Down past Moody's field.'
The sparse brambles tangled
round fences have been picked clean,
the Sheep's Bit wags
its blue-brushed head in all directions.

Wild mint, hiding in the reeds:
inhale its smell to keep us going;
footballers on the Moody's
dodge the cowpat defenders;
derelict house behind leafy walls
spotted with cream flower-pods.

Searching the juiciest and biggest,
tips of fingers pricked by reaching,
stumbling on broken blocks and plaster,
filling our boxes with stained chatter:
tasting in one the sugar and sour
the grit and slither of the afternoon.

Middle Age

Middle-age is when
you begin to get sensitive
about the crowd swearing at bald ref's.

It's when your daughter's
History homework's on Dunkirk
and she asks 'Were you around then?'

You look in the mirror every morning
glad that you're short-sighted
and haven't got your glasses on.

Certain nouns slip out of memory
to be replaced by verbs
like 'to sleep' and 'to lie'.

It's when you want time
to go rapidly to the next holiday,
yet halt completely before you die.

It's when your appalling flatulence
is exposed to your spouse
and you don't even bother to say 'Pardon!'

You acquire irritable and incurable
ailments in corners of your body
and consider using herbal remedies.

You decide you need a new challenge:
working without a tie, your naked
adam's apple is swallowed by the boss's eyes.

Middle-age is when you take yourself for granted:
treat your dreams as pieces of furniture,
get rid of them on a skip.

It's when you're addicted to routine
and you won't admit it, keep on taking it
till you O.D. on those same old scenes.

Famous Player

Larger than television
he'd drink anyone
under the floor,
gathered around him
like family and fire,
waiting on every word
the smell of scandal
stronger than draught beer:
a holiday and setting fire
to women's knickers
the team behaving just like
any other slobby trippers,
obsessed with the size of plonkers
and dubious strikers
who could go either way.
The chairman's an asset-stripper,
the manager's his dummy,
but he's City till he leaves
to sell his kicks
across the market-fields.
He talks fan-lingo
he was there when it 'went off'
at Bristol, as though
the fighting were a bomb
someone else had planted.
He's bigoted then liberated
spitting 'bent' and 'racist'
in a single sentence,
shrunk in his shoes
we just begin to argue
as he gets up to go.

Psychodahlia

Down in the darkest corridors of municipalia
is where the seed must've come from,
nurtured no doubt by a quirky computer
about the time of the Garden Festival.

It was to be Merthyr's own shrub:
a plant ideally suited to the area,
only needing to be oiled every ten years,
never losing its metallic beetroot colour.

'What should we call it?'
discussed the Parks committee:
'Mini triffid?' 'Spike drunkard?'
"ow about an ever 'ard?'

Without realising their irony,
because a stalwart councillor, after too many beers,
slipped on his way to a spaghetti
and skewered himself on the castiron cactus!

'DESTROY KILLER PLANTS!' screamed the local press,
but law and order merchants were impressed
by its vicious leaves and bought thousands
to surround the Civic Centre, schools and institutions.

Soon the forked flora had spread everywhere
threatening the soles of stray vandals,
so the Council named it 'Psychodahlia'
and the computer was made into mayor.

Gurnos Shops

An emaciated tree
clinging to its blackened leaves,
the wind snuffles chip-cartons.

The road's an aerial view
of dirt-dragging streams,
its scabs peeled off by tyres.

Clouds collect exhaust-fumes.
A man takes his beer-gut for a walk,
his wife follows on a lead unseen.

They won't climb up on plinths
where benches ought to be
and pose like shop-dummies.

Lamp-posts droop their nightly heads,
strays will do the watering.
Graffiti yells, but nobody's listening.

New Houses on Georgetown

Who lives in these new houses
with their guarding brick hedges
and blackout blinds, their rumours
of washbasins in every room?

Certainly, I know of no-one
who freely admits it,
built, as they are, on Georgetown
where networks of terraces
once crouched by the canal:
doors open to wiped feet.

Detached, their only contact
seems with Outer Space,
so I wonder if aliens
have moved in and perhaps
the red boxes are buttons
some extra-terrestrial force
will one day press.

No washing hangs displaying
vulnerability: knickers and boxers
with clownish spots, sharing a line
with slimy sports gear;
no children peep cheekily
and lob mud at passing lorries.

They turn their backs on the streets
and face each other, as if plotting
to take over. One day I'll spy on them
to see if they're from Cardiff, Avon,
or some other far-off planet.
If I feel bold, I'll climb to those boxes
and push one for the thrill of it;
I'll crowbar those dishes
to point them townward, to pick up
the lives around them, vital yet laden.

Yn y Carchar

They could kick a confession
out of Iesu himself!
The wheals on my skin
from rock-breaking remain
to score off the days.

I know I wasn't meek
my reputation rattled tongues
in hostelries, I spoke too much
when ale made my hands
spin before my face.

But though I loathed his cheek
in calling me a rag
upon his daughter's slim shoulders,
I'd never have gone so far:
oaths would throb the morning after.

Now I tread the mill and hear
every whip of the church-clock,
I could've picked a trade here,
the workings of many a lock:
one slur and the cat's unleashed on my back.

At least the pain can fade:
it's the bleeding within which destroys,
the infants' hungry wails
and women's shrieking replies,
walls where the vermin sleep.

I pace my own funeral-walk daily,
rehearsing the last light, I look down
on a plague of faces below me
drooling because it's not their plight:
I curse time with my pendulous body.

Notes
1. *Yn y Carchar* — Welsh for 'in prison'.
2. *Iesu* — Jesus.
3. In 1862, Richard Rowlands was hanged at Beaumaris Gaol for the murder of his father-in-law. He always protested his innocence. According to local tradition, he put a curse on the church-clock opposite the scaffold. To this day it has never kept the right time.

Yr Wyddfa Speaks Out!

It's summer again
and trip-trap trailing termites
carrying their backpacks
tread me down
sporting 'I've climbed Snowdon'
t-shirts: who's this 'Snowdon' anyway,
some kind of Lord?

It's rack and pinion all the way
the bumper to bumper
wanderlust like humping Nature
from grassy foothills
to flushes of heather;
get away from city-life
and breathe in fresh steam
laced with redhot cinders.

Oh! Not again! Here comes
the birdwatcher with two black eyes
jutting out, the silly old buzzard
hovering on an edge for hours
in his khaki plumage.

And there's nothing more boring
than a geomorphologist
labelling me with terms
like arrêtes and U-shaped valleys,
as the light changes
he's too busy turning pages.

Look at that snap of photographers
trying to suck the scenery
into those extended noses,
if I had the power to bring fog
swirling around my summit
to confound their art, I'd do it.

Those campers with butterfly nets,
at least they linger
to get moist with the dew
I perspire, try to listen
to my heart whose sounds
fall down to lakes, where my reflection
swims towards another winter.

Living on the Coastline

At the end of Bastion Road, of Offa's path,
the defences are mustering:
yellow mechanicals piling boulders,
sandbag parapets placed between
beach and no-man's mud-plain.

The Nova's lost its stars
and the rusted bars
make a zoo of the workmen.

The sea feigns a pool,
sewage-brown yet looking calm
as the one that had guiled
many couples with its sheen
promising weeks of Sundays.

Tide-charts graph a sickness:
aging bones crumble
with plaster from the last storm
and hands crawling from sleep
to the floor where water
could strand and wreck.

Queen Victoria and the Territorial Army
stare blankly at each other
as investigators with geigercounters
test the lying carpet silt.

It's all too quiet.
Photos and headlines no longer
reach beyond the ridge-line.
A leaf-long breeze
sounds turbulence within
and dread of another rising.

The Ghost Boy
for John Davies

Until this I did not believe:
thinking it a figure of speech,
product of too many spirits
or, simply, the heart
catching up with the mind.
Though there'd been inklings
in strange places or
                  openings in dreams.

Here, he came as I lay
facing the ceiling,
                  vivid
without sunlight
                  he stood
at the end of the bed.

Mustard-flower hair in a sash
across his forehead
                  enquiring politely
what I wanted... 'Water?'
I shook myself awake
with a horse's snortling.
His one word kept repeating
'Water... Water... Water?'
Parched, but I didn't drink again.
Childishly switched a light on.

Once a farmhouse with doors
in all directions
                  once a cafe
for serious walkers
                  the boy
waited within original stone,
his spring tone
                  sipped by finches
observing me through a glass cage
where I sat munching.

National Thinking

Why does 'Cymru'
stick to my tongue?

And the other, 'Wales',
undo its meaning
and flow naturally?

I hear the word
abused on television:
'Come-rye'
or 'Cum-roo' even,
just after the Japanese premier
has been pronounced perfectly.

I'd like to say it
without thinking.
I'd like to stop explaining
where we are in Europe
by clumsily miming
Ian Rush scoring.

I could go to London,
make ballooning speeches,
drink to bursting, die young
and be the subject of a film.
Or I could post an incendiary
for instant notices!

This principality! This region!
This province! This nation!
Let us agree on 'country',
it has the best marketing possibilities
for the Wales Tourist Board.

Leaving

She'd drive off into the night
leaving her three children
and a cheque for £100.

She was beyond the limit
yet sober as the wind
which whistled in the roof-space
like an annoying child.

The hail dug nails
into her hidden skin,
she flicked fag-ash
into an Easter egg box.

Her make-up washed off
with too much gin,
she etched in a pad
her leaving note:

'I'm away to sleep now,
the money's for the train.
I've tried and tried
but they're driving me mad.'

The black pen dug a hole
in the frosty sheets,
its marks turning to crows
which poked at the ground.

In the morning they found
a full bottle of champagne
sitting in the passenger-seat,
curled at the back she sucked her thumb.

The Human Hatchery

The naked man entered
the darkgreen promise
of the spawning-tub.

Its murky tepid water
sucked him in,
a liquid enfolding.

Lonely, except for
a tongue-lolling dog,
the distant pleas of lambs,
the inane gurgle of a pump.

This is how it began:
to the Polar ice-cap, returning.
Magnets under his skin
kept drawing his hand underwater
till it was slack with exhaustion.

There they were, the fish
of his fortune
leaping like cries of night
till they were drained
into an underground system.

He'd have no children
to be poached by education,
to be frozen
for evidence of religion.

Just this circular tank
where he'd hooked himself
nurturing salmon thoughts
from alevin to adult, infant to man,
from the bars of the gate
to cloudy currents they'd grow against.

Openings

Crows over the felt roof:
a storm-fall of acorns.

I open one window
and night flies through
in the shape
of an owl, old as oaks
its singular hoots
feathering the curtains.

One inch of the bathroom
lets in the babble
of a school yard,
drained from rocking ground
it fills the sink to overspilling.

Upstairs one Saturday morning,
just a slit and a raucous horn
clamours in, blooding
our clothes as they hang:
sleepy no more, we're bristling.

The tree's many hands tickle foundations:
pigeons feed where they emerge in the garden.

Intruder

Midnight: the panes shiver with a cold
straight from the Arctic.
Eye-lid curtains, the Close is quiet
except for his display.

We watch him on a larger screen
proceed along our street's question-mark;
peacocks still cry behind TV eyes,
his warning-lights might be their plumes.

His flashing blinks a coded message
we can't glean, his horn aggressive
in a territory he'd like to claim:
his car's armour a bullish skin.

Even out of sight we hear him
punctuating the wind. Till he returns,
steps out, squat figure in mousey colours,
scratching towards a door to be let in.

Diver-Bird

People sat up from skin-baking or shade-seeking,
children on flabby lilos stopped squall-splashing:
not a pointy snorkeller, but a diver-bird.
'Duck!' someone called, as he dipped
and disappeared underwater, emerging
liquid minutes later as no human could.
'Guillemot' I said assured, chuckling.

Grey-black, shiny as wet seaweed
his head intent for rush of a shoal,
no periscope or radar could equal
that vision: beak needling fish
leading a feathery thread up and down.
I tried to swim out, follow him,
make clicking noises to draw his attention:
he ignored my performance.

Returning home, in reference books,
I realised 'guillemot' was just as absurd.
He was elusive here as he'd been
in the bay, no silhouette fitting.
Yet I knew he'd keep re-surfacing
further and further away, stitching
more firmly because I couldn't find a name.

Sensing the Waun

1

Past the short-cropped twmps
and overgrown waste-heaps,
past the conifer-lined horizon
comes the humming:
a swarm of machines
all led by a megaphone,
quaking through strata
to where I listen.

Dust rises in the afternoon,
a whirlwind of ruddy-brown:
the motor-bees have stung
the ground and it's flaming.
The loud-hailer leader
counts them down.
The mountain's edge is lifted
and sent reeling.

2

Near to the permanent tattoo
of last year's bonfire,
I think he's a coal-figure
at first, the crown-horned bull
who seems more like a gentle gardener
than the fierce king of legend,
his coat like shining black skin
and heavyweight muscles
concentrated on chewing.

He's oblivious to the cow downslope
who tears at the sparse green
to feed her shrinking dugs:
straining under her mottled form
a black calf drags out milk
and her teats hang, pink and sore,
from his furious sucking.

3

When my daughter was twti knee-high
we'd go on expeditions over the Waun,
catching hold down the winding sheeptracks
to the print of a tramline.

There the tussocks stuck out
like elbows and the veins
of wild strawberry stalks
wound round stoney remains.

I'd mind her wobbly walk
as we searched among the cracks
for the elusive fruit:
her fingers trying to root.

They tasted disappointing, bitter and gritty,
but we nibbled like mice in barley.
She licked the red dye
but it wouldn't go away.

4

Scrabbling up the arched oak
hoping years would drop with acorns,
the rutted bark like tough skin
of a lizard, a dinosaur of childhood
where eggs were spiked:
polished pebbles within.
The urge to climb:
my feet used to fit
into cavities, into narrow v's,
we'd let the spring
monkey us up and down.
There's a ring for every wrinkle now,
my bones have been blown
and disjointed by a prevailing wind
of schedules and decisions.
My scraping foot slips
down the trunk where once
my limbs ivied, spiralling.

5

Smoke on the wind,
a scratching of claws:
I sniff but see nothing
except a scrag of crows.

I remember fields burnt after harvest,
the hard stubble sacrificed:
but this coke-oven stench
comes without reason.

Towards the tree-coursed stream
I spy the hooks of fire
snagging a rare easterly:
mockery muffled by running water.

Then another fire near the forestry
goads the sun, rushing hurriedly
through reeds and grass, its sharp points
making them writhe, bleed grey.

Firemen arrive to beat it down, police to question,
but the culprits can't be found:
black marks left on the hillside
are tar-infected lungs.

Notes
1. *Waun* — moor or common, in Welsh.
2. *twmp* — rounded hillock.
3. *twti* — small.

Odd Bird

My son's bedroom, a square safety-pane:
a chaffinch was crashing again and again
in frenzied attack, wanting in.
Disturbing, it beaked at glass
our second skin, leaving it marked
with white wounds. This spangled
bird of our temperate climate
we talked of as some portent,
some mad beast who'd get in
and whirl around a shrunken orbit
shitting on bright bedspreads:
who'd possess inside, send me scurrying
for odd means of capture, a basket
or a broom. My wife saw his dirt
on the sill as a personal insult.
I suggested the hanging mobile
might seem like a friend.
My daughter perfectly mimed
his curious eyes, searching head.
My son, less tame but more logical,
said it was his reflection.

We pulled curtains on the day
and, sure enough, by evening's return
there was the chaffinch dancing again,
prancing against the garage-window this time,
following in his solitary way
up and down, that other bird he saw
and couldn't reach, trapped forever.
His white flashes petalled
in leafy reds of his plumes;
he turned away, perturbed,
and even dropped a morsel to begin
again that exhausting display,
beating himself against an image of his own.

The Talking Shop

In the Talking Shop
they spit out bones
which an auxiliary sweeps up:
they're crushed and made into gloss
for the latest glamorous brochure.

They talk white paint, plush curtains,
flowers and plants in the foyer:
they shred leaves of Chaucer
to garnish an exhibition.

Cogs of paper push hands
and a clock somewhere
justifies its existence.
They decide to decide later.

All the pounds left over
from multi-gym exertions
are heaped on the floor
for clients to sketch
in their frequent boredom.

In the Talking Shop
originality is a luxury
nobody can afford:
and if you complain
the word-detectives soon arrest
your mouth and use it to bin
the scraped paint, dead flowers, shoddy curtains.

Catalogue for Those Who Think They Own Everything

NASA space spectacles enable you
to see the holes in the ozone layer
as they're forming and automatically
filter out the ultra-violet rays.

Acid rainproof ponchos with litmus lining
which changes colour according to levels;
no fumble lightswitch, no stain bedding,
less pressure lamp, tranquillising window-blinds.

Peel fruit in 5 seconds, polish toilet-bowl in 10,
tape that mends everything, including a broken heart;
six beautiful chokers in one as worn by Princess Di.,
talk-back plants pioneered by her husband.

Multi-vac octopus suckers for cigarette smoke,
annoying insects and the neighbours' children;
a clothes shaver, a sock de-odifier,
anti-slip shoe-grip gets rid of paranoia.

A giant helping hand for gardeners,
an extension on your penis, double-glazing for skin;
a drain buster, pet disguster, philosopher's knot,
an electric device for clearing nostrils of snot.

Learn a new language for just £5.95,
write a haiku for less than one pound;
detect radar zones over a mile away
and avoid crashes with low-flying planes.

Sonic lawn guarder repels moles harmlessly,
magnetic birds' mess collector keeps washing free;
'Don't Let The Bastards Get You Down' ties,
thermal pants with an 'Up Yours!' motif.

Walk on water — insoles to match Christ!
A revolution in home heating — who needs Marx?
Oxygen in a can, feel young in magic minutes,
no needles, no wax... ALL MADE IN BRITAIN.

Searching the Doll

Slowly pacing the beach
in age now not in sleep,
it's a cemetery
but I've come to dig.
Gulls wailing what's inside.

I'm alone again at night
in a waking trance
searching for that doll
I dropped, the blood-smirch
on its white wedding-dress.

My prints always lead back
to the cellar of that house.
A nine-month sentence stretched
to life on its camp-bed:
the memory condemned.

I chatted so readily then
hadn't learnt suspicion's martial art,
his affection the breath of air
and hands soft as powdery sand.
Soon became my jailer, my interrogator.

Buried me under his sweaty bulk
so my frenzied fingers tried
to take flight and reach up
to the single slit of light.
Dead birds washed up with the flotsam.

Jasmina in the Snow

They put out their eyes
so their crying hollows
the snow, but cannot melt
the pink remains. They couldn't wrap
a scarf of skin around
her stripped and cracked skull.

Their pokey flat shakes still
as though the shelling
carries on reverberating
long after their child...
the walls of their bones
become thinner by the second.

Jasmina was lured by the sparkle:
that light of the first fall,
that white cake icing
her fingers dipped into,
that fairground of slopes
where she sped sledging.

Her giggling glee was shot down.
It didn't reach the parapets
of surrounding hills. No radar
could possibly trace her laughter.
Yet, they must have known.

Towels cover all the mirrors:
their ice would break with tears.
A simple posy on her sledge:
red of flushed cheeks
and shining leaves palming
towards windows for release.

Jasmina in the snow.
Her trail stopped short:
a signature she'd never know.

Vedran Smailovic

People dash across our TV screens
like sheep scatting from a moorland blaze,
they'll disappear over the edge of dreams
when we ascend to sleep away the day.

But, all of a sudden, within a frame,
a portrait animated and tightly-strung:
the cellist plays on streets where lame
buildings hobble before falling down.

His slashback hair is aging rocker style,
upturned moustache makes a sign of peace;
his two faces: a pizzicato smile
and mournful vibrato of so much grief.

His audience are the pavement wreaths,
from the distance come heckles of gunfire:
the amphitheatre where he once bowed
is a frozen skip of bricks and wires.

On a thin point he gradually spins
the web-fine veins of an Adagio,
while hearing the bombs' deadening dins
and fearing for that small bridge below.

Beyond the Pale

In the Pale the planters lived,
their mansions prominent
as Viking ships, their churches
helmet-headed. They ordered
the gorse to be removed.
Their flags dripped blood
which never enriched the soil.

Some couldn't help be drawn
beyond, hearing the bodhrán's beat
of a jigging heart, tin whistle
dawning through wood and bone,
Uillean pipes sobbing with joy:
music from river and mountain.

Now you couldn't find the border:
the amber flowers blaze everywhere
and the man with native tones
could raise the whip-hand higher.

(The Pale: an area not far from Dublin City where Protestants settled in Ireland, hence the phrase 'beyond the pale'.)

Jack of Pumps

'Waaark!' he'd say 'Waaark! Waaark!'
like some belligerent crow;
he wore an oily blue forecourt coat.
His face was straight as the road
across to Barry Island,
his wit cutting into grime
like polish which revived aging paintwork.

'Y' cun go where y' likes,
but they knows y' by yer smell!'
He hated his job and most customers,
greeting them with his cawing talk,
yet with those he knew well
he'd chat like petrol overflowing
from the nozzle as the gauge went up.

Self-service threatened from round the corner,
a predator with gleaming tills.
He couldn't imagine sitting for long,
though his spine was a twisted air-pump:
pressure kept rising to his skull
so he thought it would shatter.

Tips and tokens stuck easily
to the grease of his hands
and the days' dirt would come off
with massage in thick green gel.
But in his nostrils was smog of exhaust
and in his eyes the stinging fumes,
as he bagged the takings and felt
he'd join the dodo and dinosaur soon.

Anti-resort

The white disjointed man
on brown rectangular signpost
is the only skier left
in this anti-resort of a town.

Also white on brown
is the carpet to nowhere
a once famous, now forgotten,
bespectacled celebrity opened.

The carpet's discoloured
as wool caught on wire,
the mud creeps over daily
staining its way downslope.

The Council poured money in
and it drained into the bar.
The biggest attraction since the C5:
that wheeled washing-machine!

There's talk of bobsleighs,
adventure playgrounds and FUN;
they'll erect a pit-wheel by an arcade
to spin the destiny of the final mine.

Nobody can forget that freezing night
when the snow-machine blew out flakes
which melted by the morning. Global warming
has been most cruel to Merthyr's tourism.

Jesus Runs Wild

Jesus runs wild in the mountains
around Trawsfynydd, following the lines
of dry-stone walls, down
to the deserted chapel
where he preaches 'I am the Right...'
to a congregation of dust.

Whose fault?
          Sheep are fleeing.
Whose fault?
          Cloud-shadows
mime over the slopes.
Whose fault?
          Blood from briar-wounds
drips its stops on psalms.

In its black chair the lake
constantly mourns. They've closed down
the large, symmetrical temple
where he worshipped in a mask.

His mother had gone away for a decade
to have an affair with God,
of all her children in rows
not one was him. His father
made furniture from pounds, shillings and pence,
had sung better than any bird,
while he could only starling-mimic
the sawing of wood.

Jesus runs wild to the statue
of the poet-soldier, who never wanted to fight:
wondering why they'd stopped him flying
before the war began; why the grassland
spoke Welsh at him and mocked
back, under his skin.

Man on a Skip

Rats on the lines.
A carpet of slime.
A hollow building furnished
by the stench of damp.
'Ideal Homes' sign
a sick joke
above window-blinds
of nailed boards.

Washing on the wire:
his shirt, his pants
pegged in frozen escape.
His home parked until
the next court order.

His kids looking for a bite
of warm air in the DIY centre
opposite, buzz around assistants
who try to threaten them out:
they always come back again
to sting for curse or coin.

Wearing night tied round him
with frayed rope, he scurries
to the skip between
two stumps of bridges
no bone can join.

There he lifts and shakes
and scrapes down deep
into the heaped waste
for scraps and pickings
to keep the daylight wandering.

This House, My Ghetto

It might as well be curfew here:
the pubs I can't enter any more.
It was 'Paki! Paki!', looks
like jagged, cut-throat glass
and 'You stink!'
from knuckled whites of eyes.

I was born in this town,
passed the old hospital when walking home.
I know how a girl must feel:
every stranger a criminal,
every sleight of hand a reach for steel.

The night's no camouflage:
I recall my uncle's shop,
black letters of loathing
branded across its front.
My brother and I flung like tyres,
our flesh slashed like rubber
'You don't belong... fuck off home!'
Their spittle slugging my face.

I know how a girl must feel:
even in daylight the enemy
is the man who follows and a gang
ahead send thoughts twitching.
Those bruises, insults, that blood
has stained my voice so it jitters.
Tall gate and drive, my watching window:
this house is my ghetto.

Dŵr

Clouds —
whole valley-sides covered in berries
ripe and ready for the picking,
a steep rock-face with overgrown heather,
a flock of black sheep running
to be rounded up and sheared by the wind:
water with its roots in the sky.

Rain —
the drizzly seeds of droplets sown,
the slanting sea-strewn westerlies
which turn clothing to blotting paper,
the aching storms which gravel
into bones, making you shrink and cower.

Valleys —
scooped and scoured out by laws,
people cleared away like shanty-dwellers
bossed by bulldozers, memories
left to night-writers, to bells
tolled by feeding streams and rivers,
to drought and dereliction exposed.

Reservoirs —
acid funnels of the conifers
press down soil to stop it slipping;
to trippers they seem like mirrors,
but they balance water on scales
tapping mountains for its wealth.

Pipelines —
over the border, moving like a train
with trucks of coal, like iron and steel
liquid and molten, like the feet
of all those who had to leave
muttering 'Money, money...' forced
against the gradient, longing for sea.

Chemicals —
a layer of aluminium the surface sheen,
the weight of lead its depths
and those substances meant to purify
unseen in a clear glass, lurking like radiation.

Houses —
the old person whose grasp of time
runs through knotted fingers and down the drain,
children whose minds become stagnant;
families knowing when it's cut off
water's precious as air when they choke
on the stench of their own cack,
as germs breed with cockroaches and rats.

Dŵr —
they've stolen the word, those safe-lock faces,
mispronounced it 'Door', reinforced and vaulted
below reservoirs where they've counted
profits from broken bones of village walls,
from a thirst which opens mouths
in fledgling questions to the clouds.

Acknowledgements

Acknowledgements are due to the editors of the following publications, where some of these poems first appeared: *Poetry Wales, New Welsh Review, Borderlines, Y Faner Goch, Red Poets' Society, The Cardiff Poet, Northlight, Northwords, Cencrastus, Spectrum, Fortnight, Poetry Ireland Review, Staple, Envoi, Smoke, Quartz, Hybrid, Working Titles, The Chariton Review* and *Cumberland Poetry Review*.